HOTEL SAUDADE

                                        new and old experiences

shattered trauma and love

                                    brutal fantasies

self-discoveries and U-turns

                battle between the fallen and the Most High

MICHELLE KELLY

you don't have to feel ashamed of the things you don't eagerly share with others

you are always worthy of love

LIGHTNING STRIKES THE SKY

the sun is never muted but sometimes it's blinding
when she cannot face the life force
when she cannot let it in
when the shadow's mouth is in her gut pressing on her wounds
and eating the reactions
at the same time the pallid flowers spew venom on the earth
the butterflies are rotting
the trees have turned to weapons
the only safety is in dark corners
or in the warmth of fire
her soul is trembling
her heart is full of sick
she knows the only thing to do is release the force against the shadow
that's barring its teeth
and offer it her blood

MICHELLE KELLY

DNA // BEEHIVE

you don't want your words to negatively affect me
but you never built me up
so how can I not crumble beneath your wicked ways?
your house was cold
you were cold
wrapping me in dizzying deceit
shattering my soul into multiples
like the stars in the sky I look up to and pray
to take me

~~TOXIC~~

she'll tell you she loves you and draw blood in the same breath
she'll make you want to douse your skin in fire to burn the remnants of her off you
broken memories
broken girl
if this is love, what is hate?

MICHELLE KELLY

THROUGH THE VEIL // BREATHLESS

I didn't want to leave my mother's womb
I refused to come out
when they cut her open and ripped me from her body
they found out I was drinking the blood
it was fated
that I'd be lost
fumbling around this realm
traps seen as adventures
twinkling people with hidden crimson horns
looking for safety in unsafe places

MATRIX // CODES IN SLEEP

I had a dream last night
I watched a stranger float up past the clouds
the sun was shining through whiteness
magnified
He's dead, I thought
but he came back down and said,
God is nothing you are taught it is

MICHELLE KELLY

AGGRESSIVE WING // NEPTUNE IN THE FIRST HOUSE

days spent with
doctors
therapists
psychoanalysts
after tying a belt around my neck
after trying to jump in front of a train
after slicing lines into my legs and arms
You are a danger to yourself
Take your clothes off and put on this hospital gown

laying on a bed in a small white room
the man across the hall is livid
he shrieks in a guttural voice
the veins nearly popping out of his arms and neck
pure aggression in his eyes
I fear that he's going to walk in here and strangle me
but I cannot keep my eyes off him
the rawness of him
his identity forever unknown to me
it takes seven guards to drag him back to his room
they hold him down against his will
they inject him
I am no longer afraid of him but sad for him
he's calm now
the nurse wheels my bed out of the room across from his
I don't want him to hurt you when he wakes up, she tells me
I am shocked by her kindness

sitting in the back of an ambulance
secured in a gurney
I am transported elsewhere beneath the night sky
watching the car lights of the strangers out the back window
who are free from torment
there's something about being in the back of an ambulance that

you never forget

standing on display before a stranger
opening all my vulnerable folds
shaking out my hair
bending over
lifting my breasts
because I may be hiding drugs or weapons
but the only weapon is me
my brain
these hands
Open your mouth
Swallow them
Lift your tongue

scolded for biting the skin around my nails during group therapy
sent to a private session down winding staircases and secluded doors
because they think it's a sign I am not well
but this doesn't seem like a place where you leave miraculously healed
I am sleeping in a bed a girl died in hours before
she is the reason there was an opening here
how is that supposed to feel?

Do you want to be part of an experiment?
Do you want to let us shock your brain?
How does that make you feel?
You have to swallow the pills
Find a way to do it
 We'll inject you if you don't swallow them
Chew them, then
I chew the white circular pills, the acidity so horrendous I can still taste it years later

my roommate cries at curfew in our room
because he sees demons

MICHELLE KELLY

he speaks in tongues
keeps me up all night
I say nothing
as I anticipate the wakeup call which is nurses banging on our doors
that are locked from the outside
and then stepping inside the smaller door within the door
getting us ready for more pills

another stranger sings gospel music
a manic tint to his eye
the kindest eyes
you'll ever see
everyone in here is spiritual in some way
some of them connected to a higher vibration
chanting prayers
praising Him in the most angelic voices
others have lost Him
they've taken the breath of those around them
but me
I am a nihilist
I am floating on the clouds, heart thumping faster than ever,
words spewing from my mouth too quickly for people to understand
it's like I'm on a rollercoaster blasting my favorite song
I dance in my room alone all night long
I feel free
exuberant
and then I'm visited by its twin flame
I cannot speak
the music has turned to screams
the light in my eyes has turned sullen
I am numb and disconnected
I have no energy to stand up straight
I ask The Most High to take me to Him
so He can heal me

and I won't have to suffer anymore

You do that? a boy I just met asks, sitting across from me in the common room
he's the one who told me booty juice is what we watch other people get
injected with when they misbehave
he's the one who told me this place is a game
and you have to beat the system to get out
he's a tagger
he wants to meet up when we're released
so we can create art together
guarded by nurses
he looks shocked
that someone like me would do that
Yes, I tell him
but I want to scream, *What do I look like to you?*
everyone views me in a different way
and none of their views are accurate
it confuses me
it disillusions me
who am I?
in the bathroom, while being watched by guards as I brush my teeth and shower
I find my face, morphed in the reflection
a façade of a mirror
we don't allow glass in here
someone may break it
and use it to harm themselves
or others
you see
the boy I have a crush on called me fat
but my friend says I am skinny enough to be a model
my mother says I am an ungrateful, useless, too-sensitive devil
she mocks my defaced wings
another person tells me I am stupid, reckless, slutty, a mistake,

MICHELLE KELLY

going to Hell
another person tells me I am weird
another person tells me I have big eyes
another person tells me I am perfect
another person tells me I am pretty
all these voices, all these opinions, I begin to lose my identity
how can I look so different to them than how I feel and see myself?
he takes the pencil from my grip and pries off the eraser
he frees the metal casing and morphs it into sharpness
glancing around the room to ensure the guards are not aware
he slips it into the side of my shoe
Don't let them find out, he says
They'll send you to the cushion room

after arriving home from the underworld for the second time
I dream of a wise man with a cane
thin, stoic, and short
we stop in front of a building
I watch a girl jump out of the top floor window and think, *That's me*
the prophet, guide, shaman says, *Let the old you die.*
and I try to

ARIZONA

you think you feel loneliest in a suffocating room full of people
but you realize you didn't know loneliness until all you have is
yourself and you don't even
want you

MICHELLE KELLY

SAD ANGELS // HEATHEN

I was never desperate for a halo
only desperate for destruction
I die each night at 3 AM
and rise again in the morning

UNCONDITIONAL

when someone shows you their shadow and you empathize with them, that's love

MICHELLE KELLY

ALPHA AND OMEGA

eating guilt and ruin
spitting out the seeds
always been looking for a savior
but finding abandonment in its place
I pray to Him
I beg Him
and it leaves me feeling drained
He leads me back to the hum of my heart
save yourself
save yourself
save yourself

OROOJ // THORNS TO HEAVEN'S GATE

there was once a man who said, *I don't need anything anymore*
and then he left his body
they say it's called willful dying
you don't have to wait to get ill to die
you don't have to leave your demise in another's hands
you can choose to leave at any time
some nights I can feel my soul separating from my body
my heartbeat slows down
the bed I'm lying in feels fake
the sounds, the blinds on my window, and my neighbors' voices
are from a television show
the matrix crumbles
the illusions are recognized as such
I'm about to float upwards and out of this realm
when I pull myself back down
I'm not ready yet
I choose the sun
instead of a furnace

MICHELLE KELLY

IMMORAL // LIGHT FROM THE REFRIGERATOR

people need you to bleed for them
even if they won't bleed for you

PERSPECTIVE // DEPRAVED

my mother has always yelled at me because I talk about death too much
but my therapist says I'm not scared of death because I've been so close to it

MICHELLE KELLY

TROUBLED // PRISON PLANET

the children in Cambodia get their arms chopped off
so, when they beg
they get more money
babies' ribs are poking through their skin
in Sudan
and everything else seems insignificant
immoral
hued with anger
if you're looking for Hell
you found it
millions are already doused in it
and though there may not be flames
they're burning
sinless
or
sinful
why do we allow these things to happen?
why are we unable to provide for those in need?
why haven't we learned to love each other?
this earth is a prison planet
polluted with murder, abuse, torture, unfairness
and our souls are recycled
over
and
over
and
over
with little to no
change

ADOLESENCE

on a steady diet of anger and indifference
she looks for somewhere to belong
dancing from person to person
always winding up as scorched as her cigarettes
bringing Ouija boards to parties
drinking bottles of Absolut in the morning
headphones permanent on her ears
sleep paralysis on the nights insomnia doesn't win
skipping school to get high
slipknot pouring through her headphones on the train
combat boots with every outfit
messy black eyeliner accentuating her aqueous eyes
she falls for the boys who are the meanest to her
especially the one who sacrifices living animals to Satan
in the cemetery next to their catholic school at midnight
he calls himself Morning Star
she should've seen him as dangerous as he was
but she ran toward him
aching
desperate
lonely
she's always led to the pits of Hell
smiling beneath the scalding kisses of the reaper

MICHELLE KELLY

MORTICIAN FOR THE STARS

the first time I saw suffering was when I was 5
I went to the hospital to visit my grandmother
she had tubes hooked into her body
filtering her blood
into a bucket
it made me want to throw up

my other grandmother was depressed
because of the love that wasn't reciprocated
or maybe it was something else
bottles of vodka every night and some
painkillers became her religion
I'd pick her up from the floor
fire burning my throat
promising her I wouldn't tell anyone
because being screamed at never stopped
anyone from hurting

see
we reach for things that'll hurt us
and get addicted to it
but from someone else's eyes
it looks like giving your body over to wasps
to sting you until you die
rather than slow suicide

my father smoked his lungs into ashes
just like his mother
we barely got along
even though we're both Libras
said he wished he had a son
he didn't want a second daughter
the only thing that kept us together was music
we bonded over it

HOTEL SAUDADE

when I was 8, I told him I wanted to play guitar
so, he bought me an acoustic
and some music lessons
when I graduated 8th grade, he bought me an electric guitar
a creamy silver Fender Stratocaster
that felt like a home should feel
he let me play it for hours on end
so loud he couldn't hear the tv
but he never complained
I'd give it to him and let him play
smiling
because he sounded good
as he made up his own riffs
it was the only time we weren't fighting
against each other's words and love
constantly misunderstanding each other
just like him and his father did
when he got cancer
everything changed
he became calmer
the house stopped being shook with screaming matches
between him and my mother
no more harshness
no more drowning out the sounds with music
just stillness
suffering
silent anticipation
because we wasted all this time fighting
instead of loving
he was a 6'4 Buddhist
he left home at 17 and fled to California with his friend
 he met with shamans
he stayed in strangers' homes
but he never told me the whole story
his hair started falling out from the Chemo
and I cried outside the bathroom door as he came to this revela-

MICHELLE KELLY

tion
the anger that constantly brewed inside me
heightened
but it was all just sadness
he became so weak he needed a wheelchair from the radiation
I'd meet him at the top of the stairs
holding his walker so he could balance and
enter the kitchen
eventually he became so weak he had to throw himself on the floor
and crawl into the house
my mother and I helpless
and after that
his body couldn't take it anymore
I visited him in the hospital
it was much worse than I was told
I guess keeping the information hidden was supposed to protect me
but it blindsided me
and made everything more intense
leaving me feeling more lost
he was lying in the bed and could no longer breathe
strapped with oxygen
no longer able to speak
moving his hands made him even more exhausted
that's the last time I saw my father
the only thing I did was weep
I never got to say goodbye

not too long after
my grandfather had a heart attack
he ended up in the hospital
his daughter said he's not doing well
so, I went to see him
his frail body naked
his eyes closed
his body shivering

curled up on his side
mumbling incomprehensible phrases
that's the last time I saw him
before he got sick, I'd deliver his mail to him
one time he was touching himself
and didn't stop even though I was there

I've always been drawn to graveyards
I'd read the headstones
sit underneath a tree
and read poetry
it was peaceful there
we kept each other company
and after burying loved ones
or burning their bodies
I thought
we should toss the dead people in the dirt
and let trees grow in their wake

MICHELLE KELLY

R.E.M // 5 A.M

we are made of moon dust
we are vibrating
with bones like starlight
reflections of you are everywhere
in the veins of leaves
in the pulse of white roses
in lightning
our brain cells are akin to the galaxies
so, the next time you feel alone
pitiful
disconnected
pick up a leaf
gaze up at the night sky
put your hand on your heart
you are alive
you are God's organic creation
and that pulsing of your heart is telling you it
loves you

VESSEL

with her whiskey-tainted soul and wounded wings
fire escapes her throat
bats rise from the shadows
the devil holds up her body like an exorcism
as crows devour her flesh

MICHELLE KELLY

VIOLENT LOVE // BROKEN NESTS

showers don't remove the dirt from her soul
where are we supposed to drop the weight?
when the scars never stop bleeding
and the bestial constellations
turn hollow
while your prayers become obscene

TANGLED VEINS // MIDNIGHT LABOTAMY

her heart swells to explosion
with her body covered in papercuts
she stores knives inside of her crevices
but it turned her blood bitter
she's unearthly
with her slime-coated prayers
to be experienced
not just looked at
but devoured
feasted
known

MICHELLE KELLY

IT BLOOMED IN WINTER

this wound is yours
only your name
can heal it

THE MORGUE // APOCALYPTIC

some days it feels like I'm courting demons
so I drink in the cataclysm
and watch the desiccated butterflies
haunt ghosts
while they look for a salve for survival

MICHELLE KELLY

SATURN RETROGRADE

spring is the epitome of emerging after a dark night of the soul
the earth eats itself
it pours its tears onto the flowers
soaks the soil
it's infested with periods of silence
and monstrous thunder
because it doesn't ask for peace
or
softness
it thrives in tragedy
just like
me

CEMETERY FOR LOVERS

when we met, our shadows held hands
and our souls sighed in relief

MICHELLE KELLY

BANKRUPT LOVE

your voice is my home

SPONTANEOUS COMBUSTION // DANCING ON MARS

she walks through the cloudless veil
hypnotized by the clusters of stars
she reaches for the divine
but gets swept up by a sour eclipse
the path is adorned with bleeding daisies
she sees herself in them
as they both got left behind
she waits for the sun to warm her mouth
and pick her up
to drop her in a vase
using her blood
to stop
osmosis

MICHELLE KELLY

SHAMELESS // DON'T BE ASHAMED

the sun, like overripe fruit
her smile, rageless
her love, like lightning
when the night comes
her body blooms like darkness
her chest is pried open like onyx drapes
she's most herself
with the stars
tucked inside of her
her human nature chiseled
taken over by everything ethereal
intoxicated from drinking the crescent moon
and stars

UNCOVERED CORPSE

with her eyes pressed shut
she leaves one dimension
and enters another
her body is paralyzed
but she's conscious
as the disjointed shadow creature hovers over her
unable to wake up
or vanish
she realizes that the demons lurking
in the astral
who tie up her heart
and gut
with invisible thread
were once humans
on earth

MICHELLE KELLY

TO DIE IS TO BE BORN

maybe there is relief in knowing
death is waiting for you

RAZOR UNDER MY PILLOW

the worst part about being alive is there aren't any answers
just echoes
leading you back to yourself

MICHELLE KELLY

FREUDIAN DREAMS

mother on her knees before daddy
her gags escape beneath the crevices of the bathroom door
because he has aggression on his tongue
and
alcohol as his religion

LOVE IS PAIN

it's like the taste for harm
was built into me
I was born with it
to offer my body up to people who want to spit on it
use it
unleash their fury
and I allow it
willingly
as an act of love
take me
use me
hurt me
because I understand you need to

I had a crush on this boy
we were by the industrial buildings near my house on Halloween
and he was mad about something
manic, really
and out of all the boys and girls around
he chose me
to throw against a brick wall
drawing blood from the wound on my head
and when we got a bit older
he was my first kiss

I was programmed to be a victim
a martyr
a slave
I was never allowed to stand up for myself
they silenced me
fists hitting my head
screams overpowering me
sore scalp from being dragged on the floor by my hair
fingers stepped on because I am there to be taken

MICHELLE KELLY

I am not my own
I am everyone else's to be what they need me to be
a peace offering
a human place to release their rage
It's okay
I understand
I love you

WOUNDS ARE ROSES

sick with sin
sick with love
floating inside this noxious body
weary from bittersweet daydreams
we collect these relationships
experiences
moments
and they all turn into confessions
the thought of teething
all those years ago
feels like a season to weep

MICHELLE KELLY

WAKE UP

life is relentless grieving

THEY SAY EVEN HELL IS HOLY

I'm tired of harboring rage
and battling invisible forces
I saved a stranger from a burning building in my dream last night
the suffering never ends
I missed my invitation to feast on love

MICHELLE KELLY

YOU WILL NOT BE MISSED

when I was a little girl
I'd always plan my escape
to flee from this house
with my suitcase full of
loneliness

FAIRYTALE

love is the darkest mission of all

MICHELLE KELLY

PUT THE KNIFE DOWN // I AM A HOME

love drips from her lips
as she looks at the stars quivering in the sky
the bloody hearts thrashing in our chests
should have a ring like Saturn
because they are planets beating inside of us
we allow others to live on the planet
and when they die
or leave
we hold their essence there
nurturing who they once were

RAPTURE

looking for a cure on your tongue
a poem in your skin
a prayer in your voice
with a gun pressed to both of our temples

MICHELLE KELLY

ALL BECAUSE I HIDE MY TEARS

she hurts me and tells me
you are strong
you can take it

SERENADED AT MIDNIGHT

come closer
you are never close enough
one day we will part
and I won't know you anymore

MICHELLE KELLY

HEDONISTIC CRIES

spume pouring from your mouth
sweet earth secretions fading around the world
the oceans never sleep
they are hunters, gathering secrets
they never complain
and humans are waiting with a loaded barrel
interrupting silences
complaining about raindrops
and desires

A SECOND CHANCE // FALSE ALARM

fearless waves devoured her body
prying, begging, provoking her young, fearless organs
this is a sacred place
the storm's flame brought her in
tides toss her around
sand thuds against her skin
her rhapsodic soul is on the verge of non-constraint
this is it
a heavenly surrender
awaiting God's face

MICHELLE KELLY

THE PORTAL // BLOODY MARY

you stare into the mirror long enough
for the clouds to turn crimson
and your face to turn sinister
entirely unrecognizable
what exists between the veil
is the opposite of home
portals are everywhere
and you look into them all the time
black cubes
black screens
the spirits watch you as you watch them
you give them shelter
a vessel
blinded by the entertainment they provide

SELF-HARM

when you compare yourself to other people
you are hurting yourself
when you tell yourself you aren't good enough
you are hurting yourself
all you need to be is the best you can be
you don't need to be the prettiest, smartest, or most talented in the room
but you need to be the prettiest, smartest, most talented version of yourself
you can be in the room

MICHELLE KELLY

ADULTHOOD

take bites out of my melancholic brain
and swallow them
it's a vengeful act
but it can be romantic if you want it to be
we have all these choices now
we choose how to feel
when to die
who to kill
when we sleep
when we put ourselves in danger
all these choices
what do *you* choose?

MOTEL 666

In the crusty motel right off the highway
I lay in a bed so many have laid in before me
so many experiences
scents
emotions
paths
trapped in the vents and the bed
heartbroken
happy
sick
angry
the thoughts they had clinging to the walls
their DNA on the pillows
here I am
devouring them all

MICHELLE KELLY

BROKEN WINGS

depression is trauma turned into a demon

HOME

it's the kind of love that fills you like rain

www.ingramcontent.com/pod-product-compliance
Lightning Source LLC
Chambersburg PA
CBHW050311220526
45465CB00005B/1939